MY FRIEND JAMAL

STORY AND
PHOTOGRAPHY BY
**ANNA
MCQUINN**

ARTWORK BY
BEN FREY

ALANNA BOOKS

Now we talk all the time – except when Miss Hall makes us sit apart – for talking too much!

Sometimes Jamal comes to my house. His mum told my mum that he's not allowed to eat sausages, because he's a Muslim. He can't drink milk either, because he has eczema.

Sometimes I go to Jamal's house.
It smells different to ours because his mum
cooks with special spices and they float
around the house.

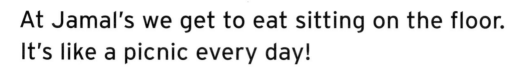

At Jamal's we get to eat sitting on the floor.
It's like a picnic every day!

My favourite thing to eat at Jamal's is
Sabayad, which is a kind of pancake.

When we have spaghetti, Jamal's mum puts a banana in it — which sounds weird but tastes excellent.

I asked my mum if we could have banana in our spaghetti at home. She says she'll think about it.

When we are at Jamal's house, mostly we play at being superheroes. Jamal has a cool outfit he got for his birthday. Usually he wears the suit and I wear the cape...

Sometimes it's the other way around.

At my house, we play basketball. I'm always Tony Parker — he's the best player ever. Jamal is Luol Deng! He has a real jersey he got from his cousin in Amsterdam.

When we're big, we're going to play on the same team and live in a huge house and have a monster car like the ones on TV. I want it to be an SUV and Jamal wants a Hummer – we argue about it all the time.

Sometimes when I'm at Jamal's house, his mum goes into her bedroom and prays. She prays at one o'clock and six o'clock.

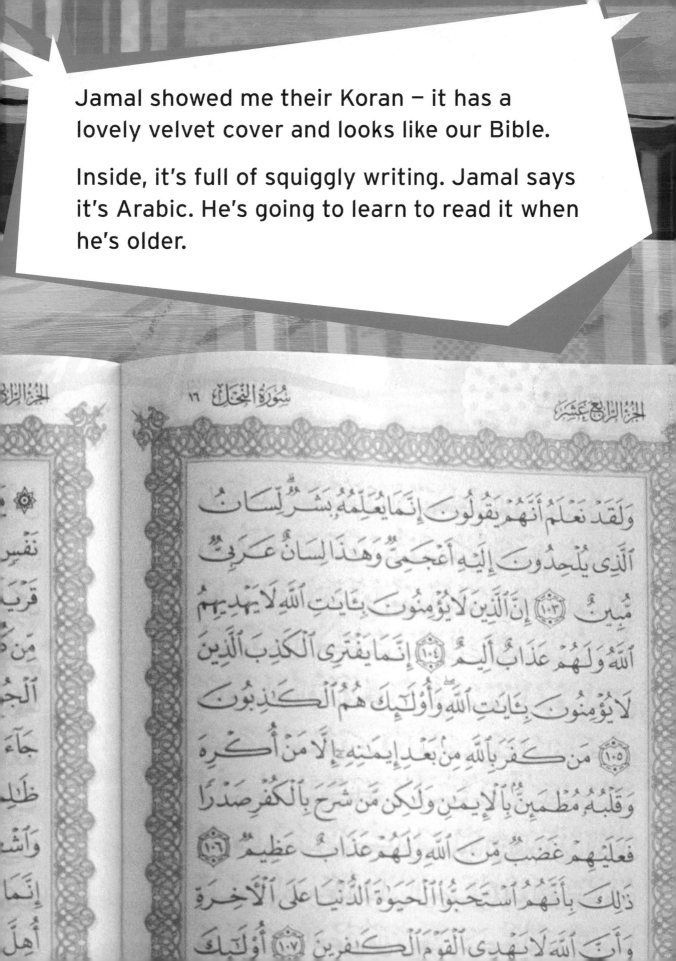

Jamal showed me their Koran – it has a lovely velvet cover and looks like our Bible.

Inside, it's full of squiggly writing. Jamal says it's Arabic. He's going to learn to read it when he's older.

Jamal's mum and dad were born in Somalia, in Africa — but a lot of fighting started and people were getting killed. It was very dangerous, so they had to escape.

They came here to find peace.

Jamal says sometimes his mum gets very lonely for Somalia. He says she misses the sunshine and her mum – but she doesn't miss the fighting.

There wasn't always fighting. When she was little, she and her sisters could play outside. She had lots of friends and a bike.

At the end of the year, we had a big concert at school. All our mums and dads came. Jamal and I sang a song together. Then we had a party.

All the mums had cooked different things. My mum made banana bread. It's my nan's secret recipe. Jamal ate six slices!

Everybody got dressed up for the party.
Jamal wore a wicked jacket with shiny buttons.

I wore the new shirt my dad bought for me.

I met one of Jamal's aunts at the party. She was wearing jeans and a sweatshirt.

I thought if you were Somali you had to wear Somali clothes, like Jamal's mum, but his aunt said you can still be a Somali in jeans!

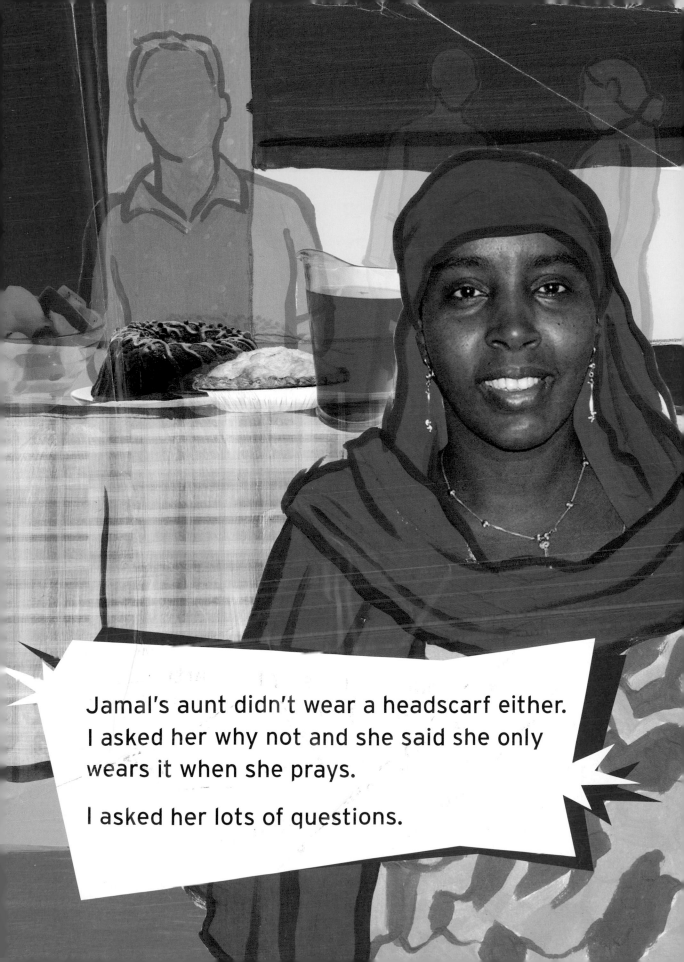

Jamal's aunt didn't wear a headscarf either. I asked her why not and she said she only wears it when she prays.

I asked her lots of questions.

Jamal's mum knows Somali and Arabic and Italian, which is a lot! But she had to go to college to learn English.

Now she is learning computers. Sometimes Jamal has to help her with her homework. I think it's funny for a boy to help his mum.

Jamal went to Canada this summer to visit his cousins. I wasn't sorry for him then. I was jealous — I've never been on an aeroplane.

I want to say thank you to Milgo and Ayan for answering my many questions and to Shamsa for being my sister and my teacher. I want to thank Jamilla for being lovely and Jamal for lending us his name. Thanks to Suzan, Sulaika and Yvonne for their help and Toni at Annick for her endless patience.

I want to thank the families who appear in the book — Anne-Marie and Kevin, Shamsa and Hassan — for their hospitality and patience with my constant presence in their homes. Finally, I want to thank two wonderful boys: Liam is my new friend and Mohamed has been an inspiration for a long time.

This book is dedicated to Brian, the little piece of home I brought with me.

All photos by Anna McQuinn and artwork by Ben Frey unless specified otherwise: skyline, pasta, curtains: © Ben Frey; notepaper: © istockphoto.com/Michael Henderson; student at desk, superhero, women and bicycle, sandwiches, pierogies, buns, cake, fruit salad, water bottle, cupcakes,: © istockphoto.com; racing flag: © istockphoto.com/Ryan Burke; BMX rider: © istockphoto.com/Robert Simon; toy car: © istockphoto.com/Krzysztof Krzyscin ; rhinoceros: © istockphoto.com/Liz Leyden; pizza: © istockphoto.com/Vasko Miokovic; sandwich: © istockphoto.com/Kelly Cline; pots: © istockphoto.com/Stuart Pitkin; Hummer: © istockphoto.com/Richard Scherzinger; SUV: © istockphoto.com/ Avesun; Koran: © istockphoto.com/Steven Allan; palm trees (closeup): © istockphoto.com/Pierrette Guertin; rubble pile: © istockphoto.com/Aaron Kohr; photo illustration of Somali soldiers, Mogadishu (1528421): © AP Photo/ Karel Prinsloo; kids playing soccer: © istockphoto.com/Donald Gargano; grass: © istockphoto.com/Kutay Tanir; tree: © istockphoto.com/Christine Balderas; chestnut tree: © istockphoto.com/Andrey Prokhorov; girl running, girl walking, palm trees (background), blue flower fabric: © istockphoto.com/Peeter Viisimaa; Fiat: © istockphoto. com/Loic Bernard; audience (two photos): © istockphoto.com/Don Bayley; samosas: © istockphoto.com/Laurent Renault; juice: © istockphoto.com/Ronald Bloom; cookies: © istockphoto.com/April Martine; donuts: © istockphoto. com/Saskia Massink; chips: © istockphoto.com/Kati Molin; red balloon: © istockphoto.com/Clayton Hansen; pie: © istockphoto.com/Dawn Liljenquist; African street scene: © istockphoto.com/Raimond Siebesma; polar bear: istockphoto.com/Petr Mašek; cacti: istockphoto.com/Mark Coffey; dolphin: © istockphoto.com/Graham Heywood; toy plane: © istockphoto.com/Daniel Timiraos

First published in the United Kingdom in 2008 by Alanna Books
46 Chalvey Road East, Slough, Berkshire,
SL1 2LR, United Kingdom

© 2008 Anna McQuinn (text and photos)
© 2008 Ben Frey (artwork)
First published and originated in 2008 by Annick Press, Canada
Cover and interior design by Irvin Cheung / iCheung Design, inc.

www.alanna.demon.co.uk

ISBN: 978-0-9551998-1-3

Printed and bound in China